Educational Adviser: Lynda Snowdon
Designer: Julian Holland
Picture researcher: Stella Martin
Artist for Contents pages: Julian Holland

Photo credits:
J. Allan Cash, 8-9, 14-15; Aspect Picture Library, 4-5, 24-25, 30-31; Australian Information Service, 22-23; Barnaby's Picture Library, 12-13; Douglas Dickins, 6-7; Alan Hutchison Library, 20-21, 28-29; ZEFA, 10-11, 16-19, 26-27
Cover picture: ZEFA

© 1986 by Dillon Press, Inc. All rights reserved

Dillon Press, Inc., 242 Portland Avenue South
Minneapolis, Minnesota 55415

This edition published by Dillon Press by arrangement with Macmillan Children's Books, London, England.
© Macmillan Publishers Limited, 1983

Library of Congress Cataloging-in-Publication Data

Karavasil, Josephine.
 Houses and homes around the world.

 (International picture library)
 Summary: Brief text and photographs introduce the many different types of homes of people around the world.
 1. Dwellings—Juvenile literature. 2. Architecture, Domestic—Juvenile literature. [1. Dwellings. 2. Architecture, Domestic] I. Title. II. Series.
NA7120.K19   1986   728   86-2073
ISBN 0-87518-336-0

International Picture Library

Houses and Homes Around the World

Josephine Karavasil

DILLON PRESS, INC.
Minneapolis, Minnesota 55415

Contents

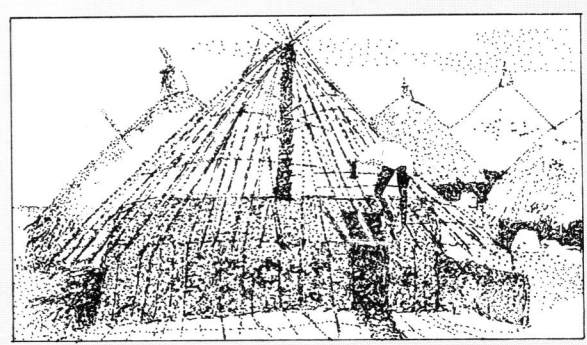

10 House-Building in India

4 Thatched Houses in Japan

12 Washing Clothes in Old Delhi, India

6 A Floating Town in Hong Kong

14 House Boats in India

8 High-Rise Apartments in Singapore

16 A Street in Charleston, USA

18 Slums in Rio de Janeiro, Brazil

26 Ghorfas in Medenine, Tunisia

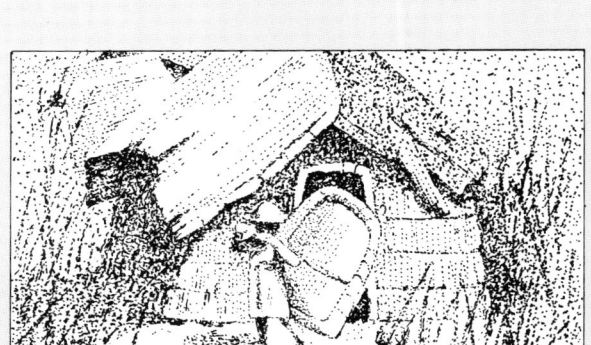
20 Houses Made of Rushes in Peru

28 Somali Camp in Africa

22 Wooden Houses in Brisbane, Australia

30 Town on the River Neckar, Germany

32 Places Featured in this Book

24 Watching Television on an Island in the Pacific

Thatched Houses in Japan
People have built houses like this for hundreds of years. The walls are made of wood, paper and bamboo. The roofs are made of straw. Sometimes

there are earthquakes. The ground trembles and shakes. You would not be very safe in a house made of bricks. But the walls of these houses just move gently and do not fall down.

A Floating Town in Hong Kong
All the people in this town live on the water. They call their boats "junks" or "sampans." They usually use them for fishing. But today is a holiday. People

have hung up flags for the Chinese New Year. All the children are wearing their best clothes. They are playing on the boat. Can you see the restaurant on the right of the picture?

High-Rise Apartments in Singapore
There are homes called apartments in these tall buildings. The apartments are built one on top of another. This means that many families can live

in each building. Homes like these are called high-rise apartments. People had to bring the concrete here in big trucks to make the apartments. Can you see where the washing is hung out to dry?

House-Building in India

In many parts of India people are very poor. This fisherman has made his house out of mud. Now he is putting on the roof. He is building the shape out of

sticks. Then he will cover it with palm leaves. It is usually very dry here. Sometimes there are storms and floods. When this happens the houses may be damaged.

Washing Clothes in Old Delhi, India
So many people live in this city that there are not enough houses for all of them. Only a few of the houses have water from a faucet. But the large brick

well has water in it. The man has just pulled a bucket of water out of the well. He will fill up his bowl. The women are washing the clothes and hanging them up to dry.

13

House Boats in India

These people take their house with them when they move, like a snail and its shell. They live and play in the boat. They also work from it. They carry things

that people need, like clothes and food, up and down the river. People come to the boat to buy what they need. The house boats in India are usually made of wood.

A Street in Charleston, USA
These neat, white houses are quite old. When people first came to this part of America from Great Britain, they found forests full of trees. They used the

wood from the trees to build their houses. Today, people usually build the houses with bricks or concrete, but there are still some wooden houses like these.

Slums in Rio de Janeiro, Brazil
Many people live in this city. Because there are not enough houses for all of them, some of them make shelters out of things other people throw away.

There is no room to grow food. There are no faucets or drains and sometimes people get sick. But these boys are lucky. They look well and strong. The dog seems to have a lot of energy, too.

Houses Made of Rushes in Peru
This house stands on an island in the middle of a lake. Tall, green rushes grow near the water. They are straight and strong. When they are dried, the

people use them to make walls, roofs and doors. This little girl lives in the rush house. She is carrying one of the rushes. Her hat helps to keep the sun out of her eyes.

Wooden Houses in Brisbane, Australia
There are hundreds of trees on the hills in this part of Australia. People cut down the trees and use the wood to make their houses. They paint the iron

roofs in different colors — red, green and grey. Sometimes it rains heavily and the river floods. But the people are safe. The houses are high up and the water cannot reach them.

Watching Television on an Island in the Pacific
This family is watching its favorite television program. Can you see the boy lying on his stomach? The hut shades the people from the hot

sun. Sometimes it rains and they can roll down blinds made from leaves. This hut is not their home but the house they live in looks exactly the same. It stands on a platform of stones to keep it dry.

Ghorfas in Medenine, Tunisia
These houses are called "ghorfas." The weather here is very hot and the sun bakes the ground dry and hard. People wear long, loose clothing to keep

cool. Inside the ghorfas, the thick walls keep out the strong heat. Families build one room on top of the other. They live downstairs and store their things upstairs.

Somali Camp in Africa

These people travel from place to place and build a new house each time they stop. It is just like putting up a tent. First, they make a shape out of twigs. Then

28

they cover it with anything they can find. Here, they have used straw, old sacks and animal skins. They can find these things anywhere they go. The Somalis keep herds of camels and cook on open fires.

Town on the River Neckar, Germany
The bright sun is shining on these houses. The pretty awnings over the windows look like eyelashes. They keep the houses cool. When it rains, the water

runs off the sloping tiled roofs. People here like to live near the river. Big barges bring the food, fuel and the things they need for their work. The barges come from towns nearby.

Places Featured in this Book

1	Thatched Houses, Japan	8	Slums, Rio de Janeiro, Brazil
2	Floating Town, Hong Kong	9	Rush Houses, Peru
3	High-Rise Flats, Singapore	10	Wooden Houses, Brisbane, Australia
4	House-Building, India	11	Watching Television, Pacific Island
5	Washing Clothes, Delhi, India	12	Ghorfas, Medenine, Tunisia
6	House Boats, India	13	Somali Camp, Africa
7	Street, Charleston, USA	14	Town, River Neckar, Germany